This journal belongs to:

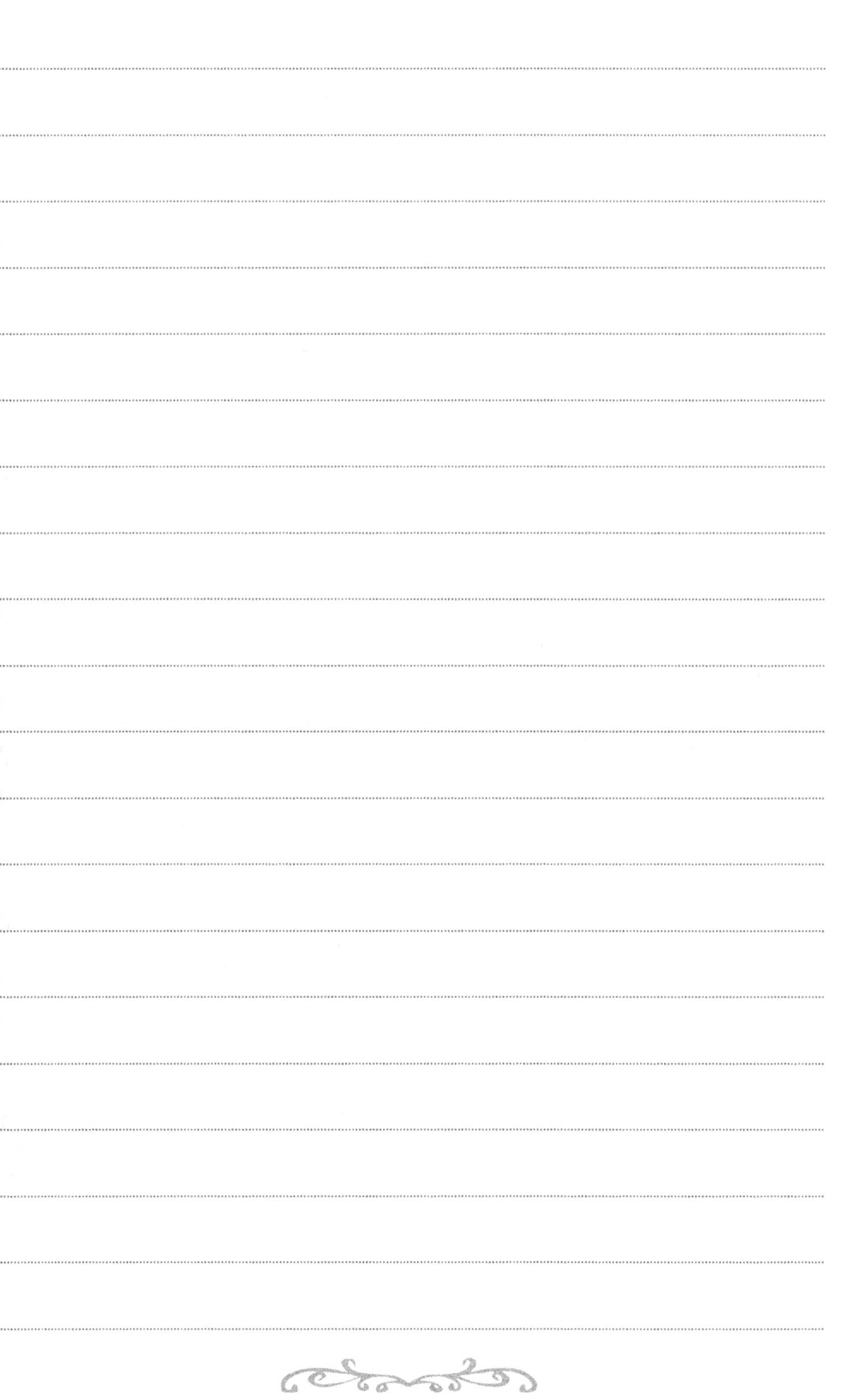

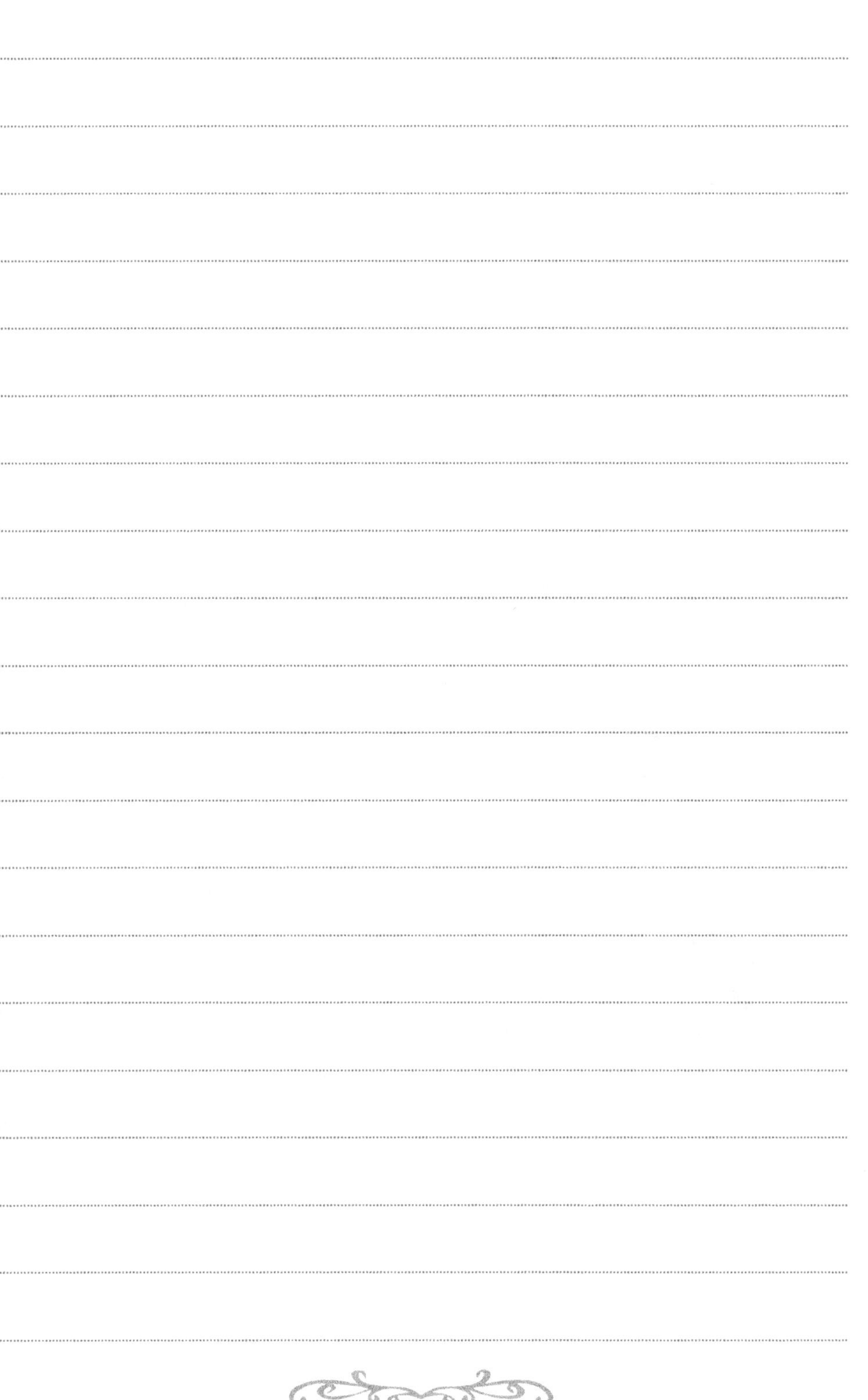

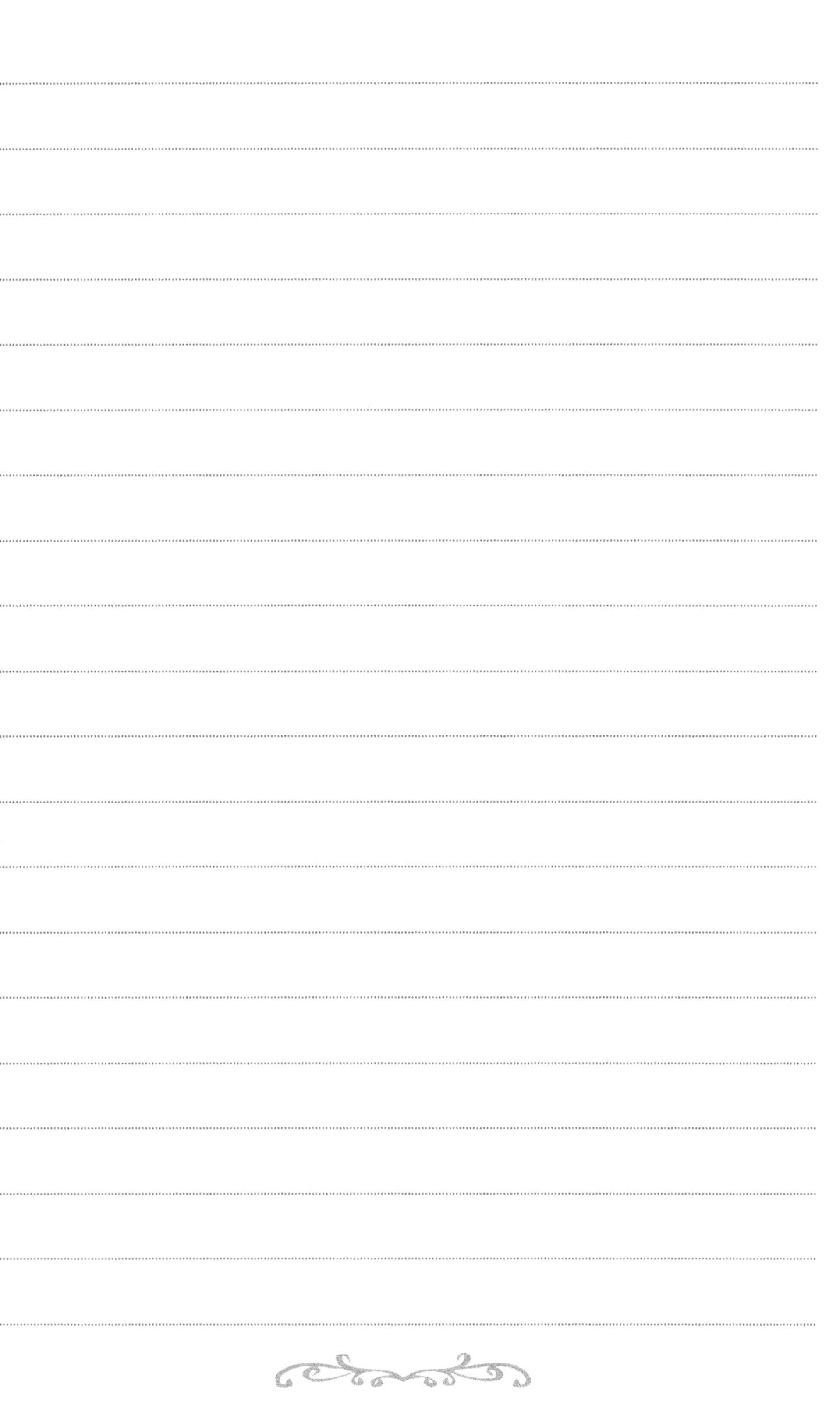

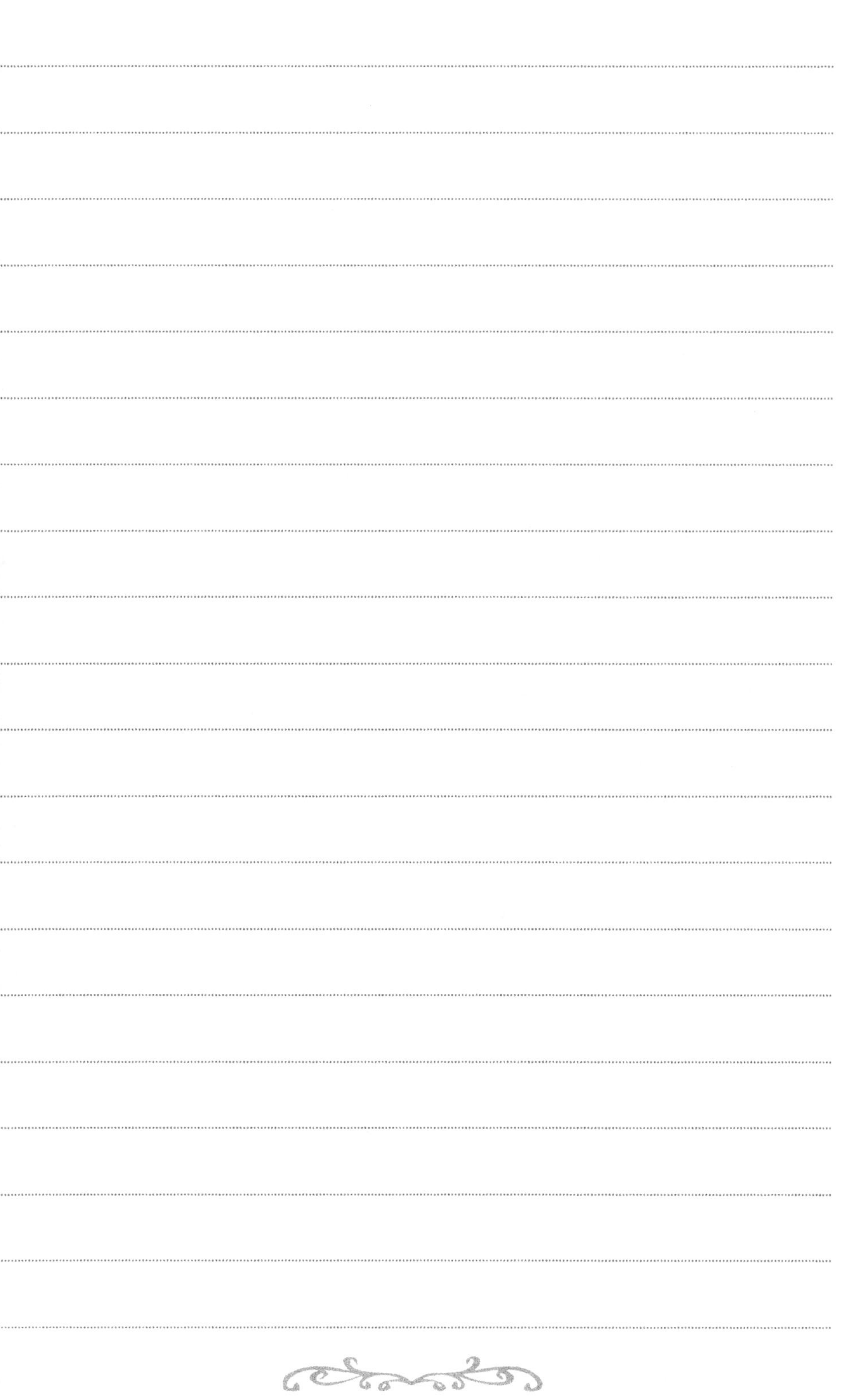

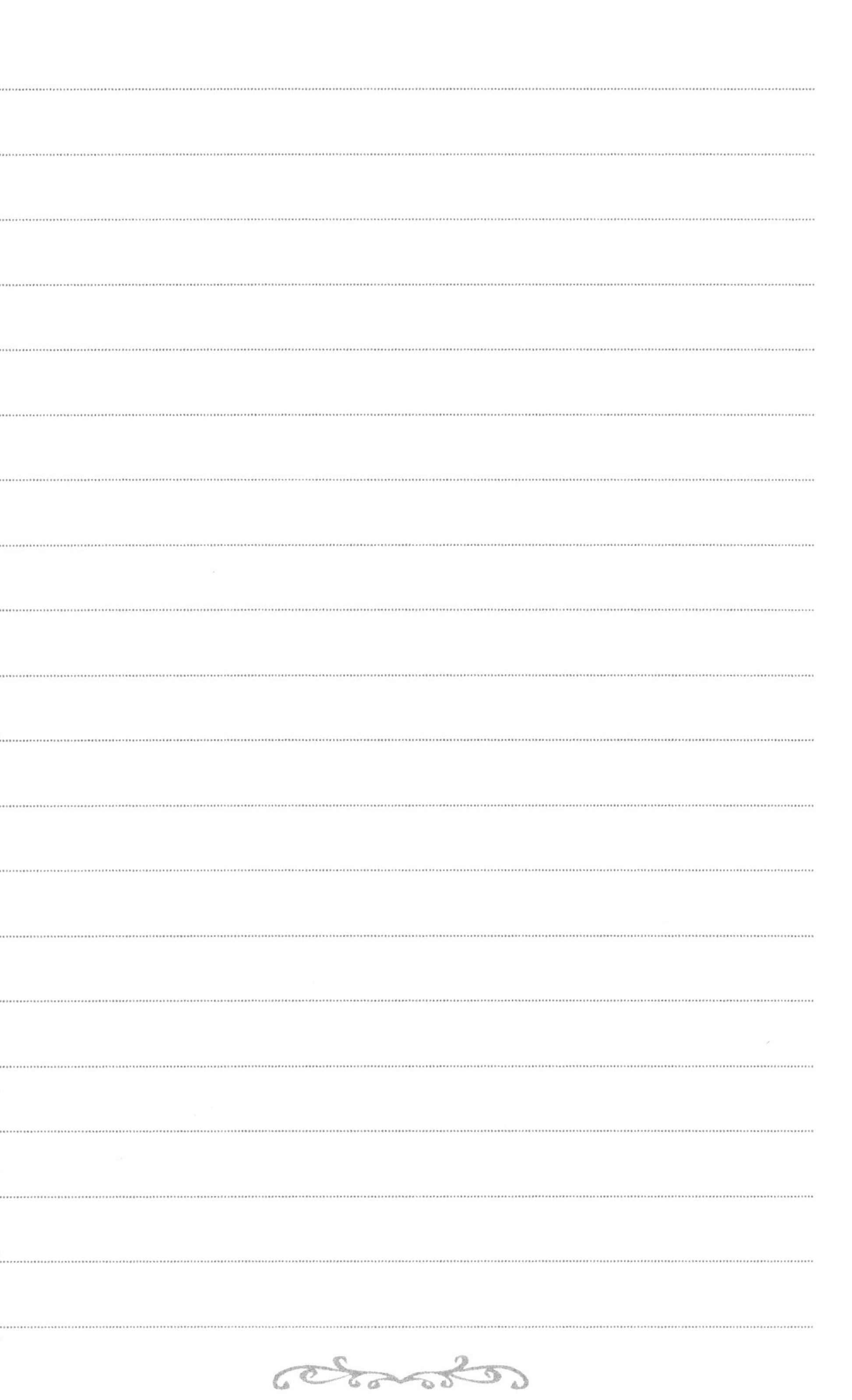

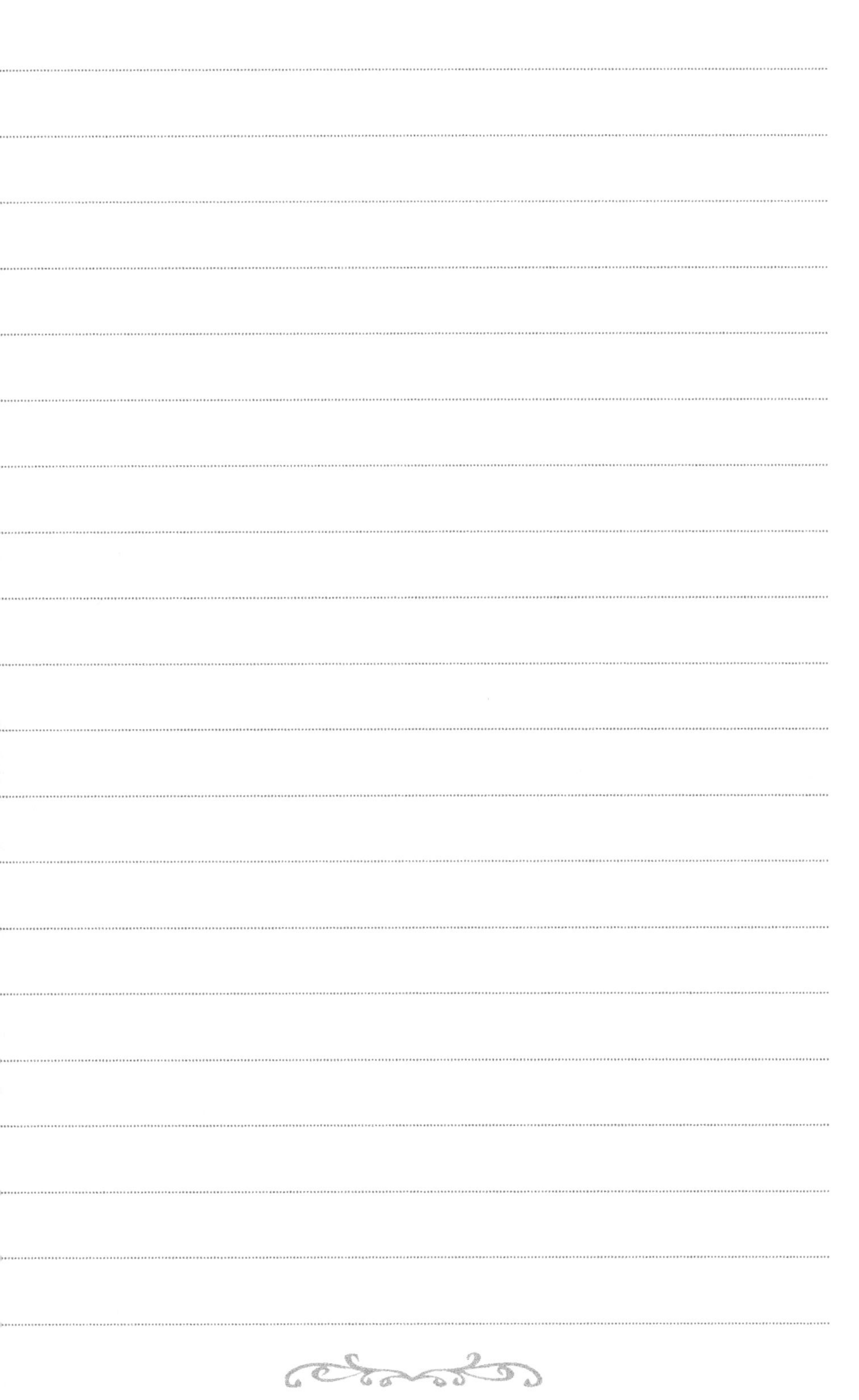

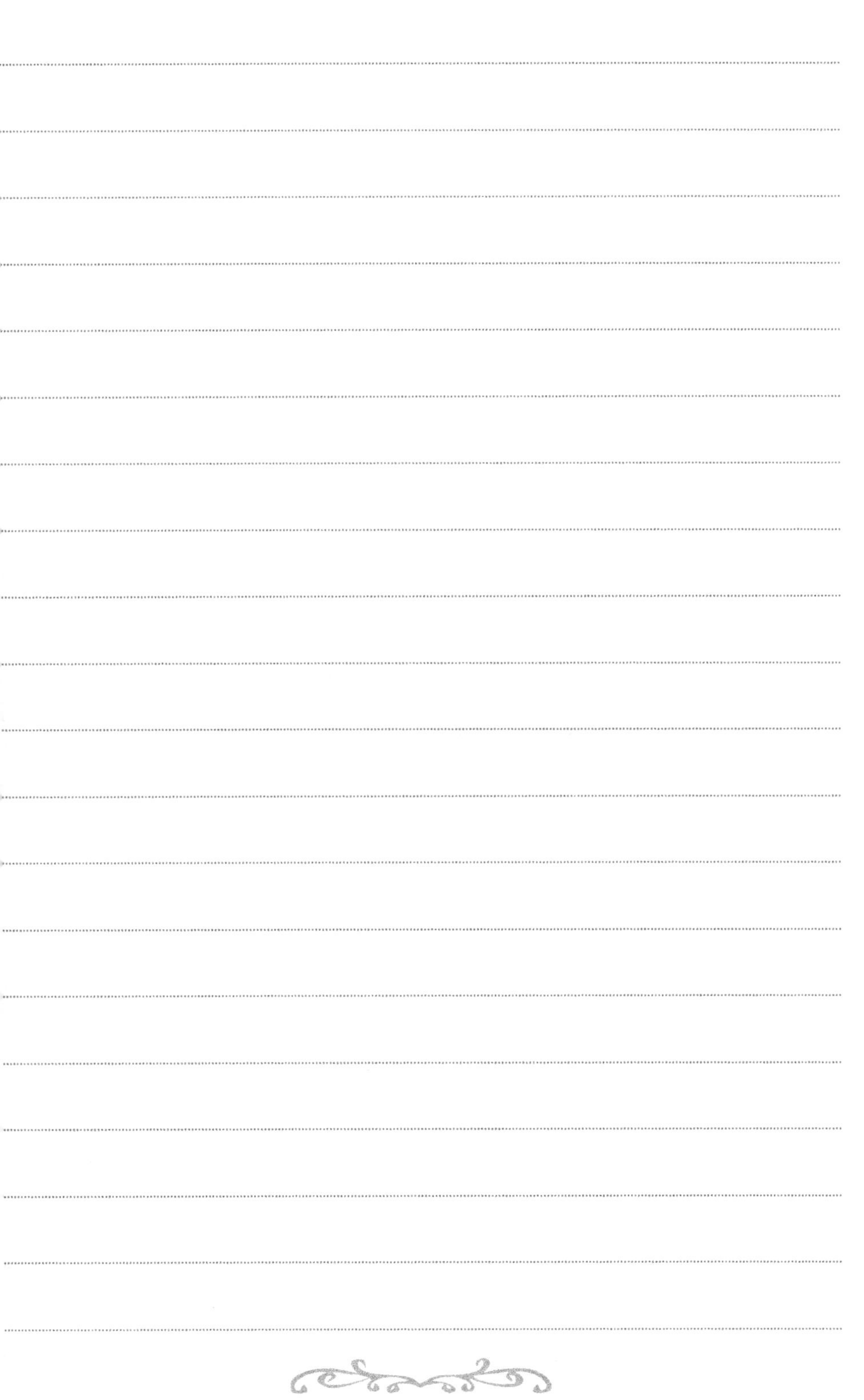

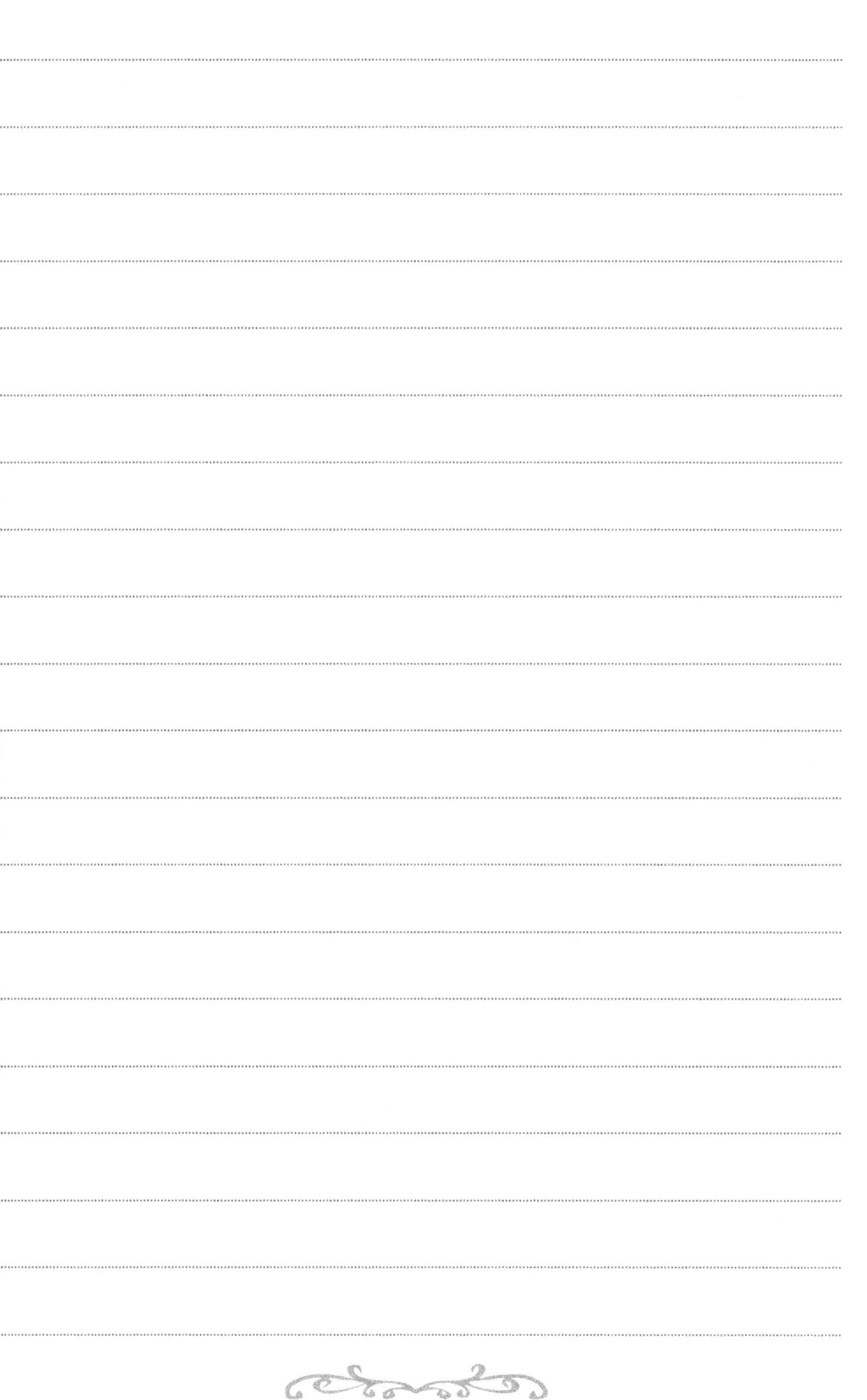

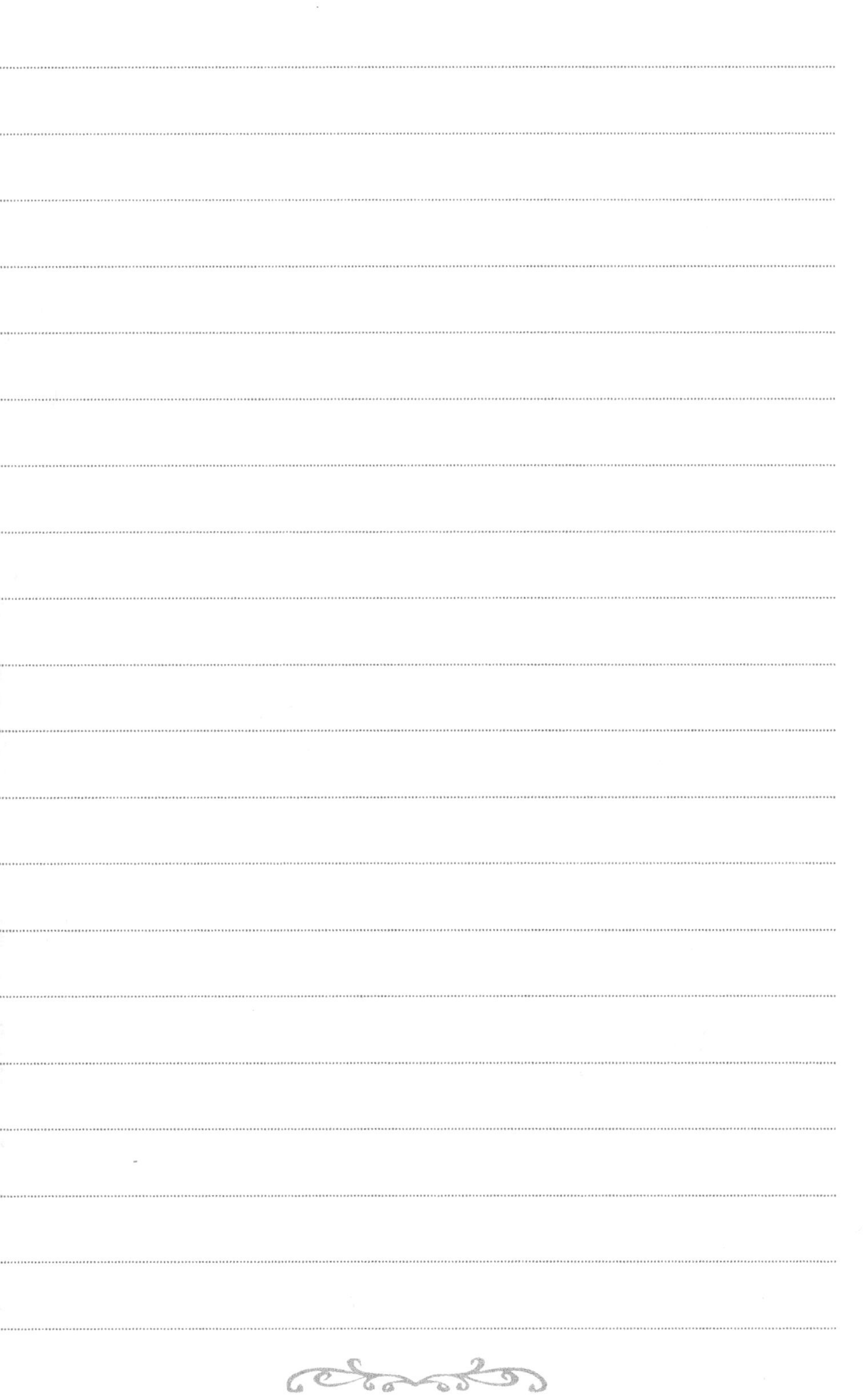

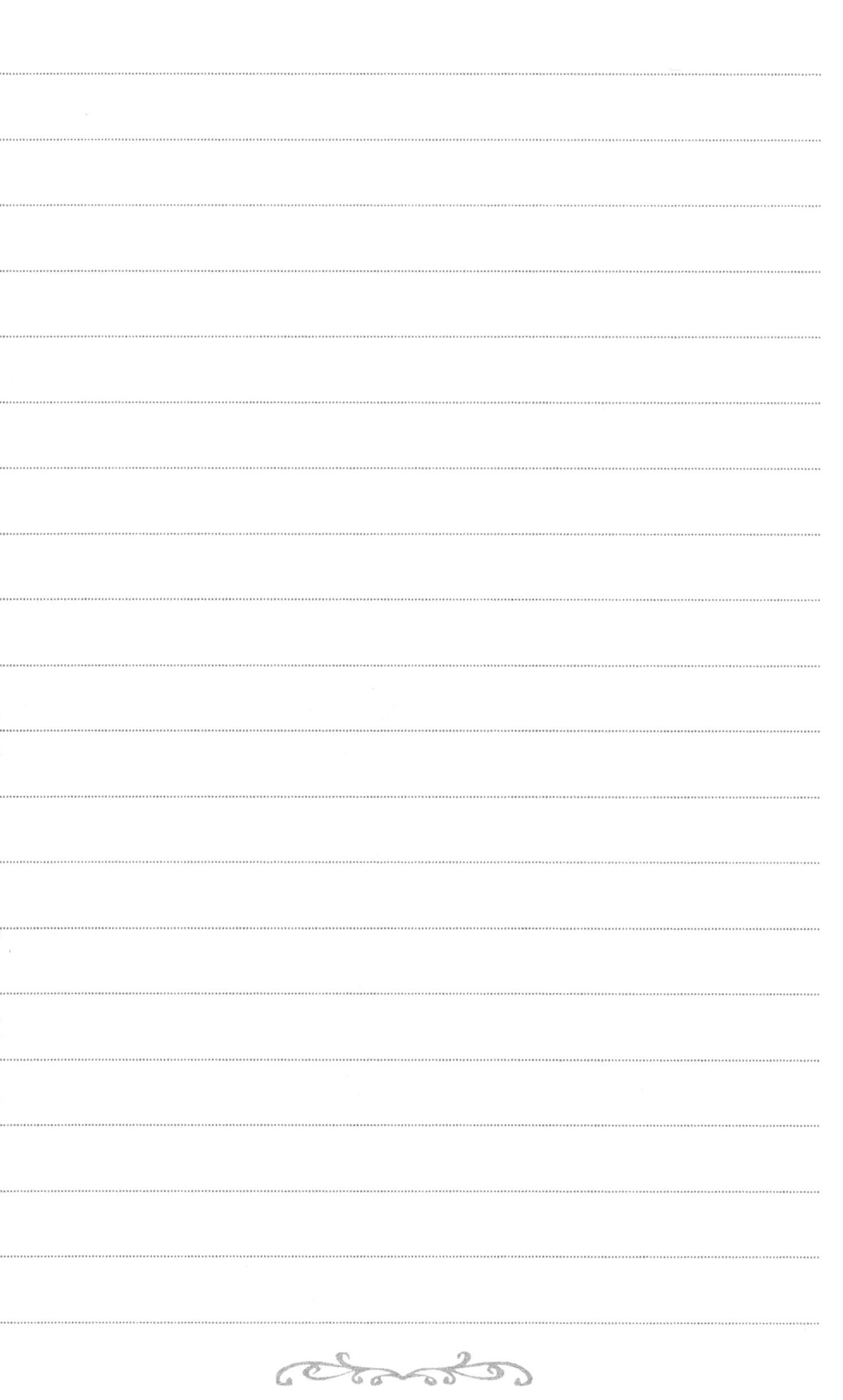

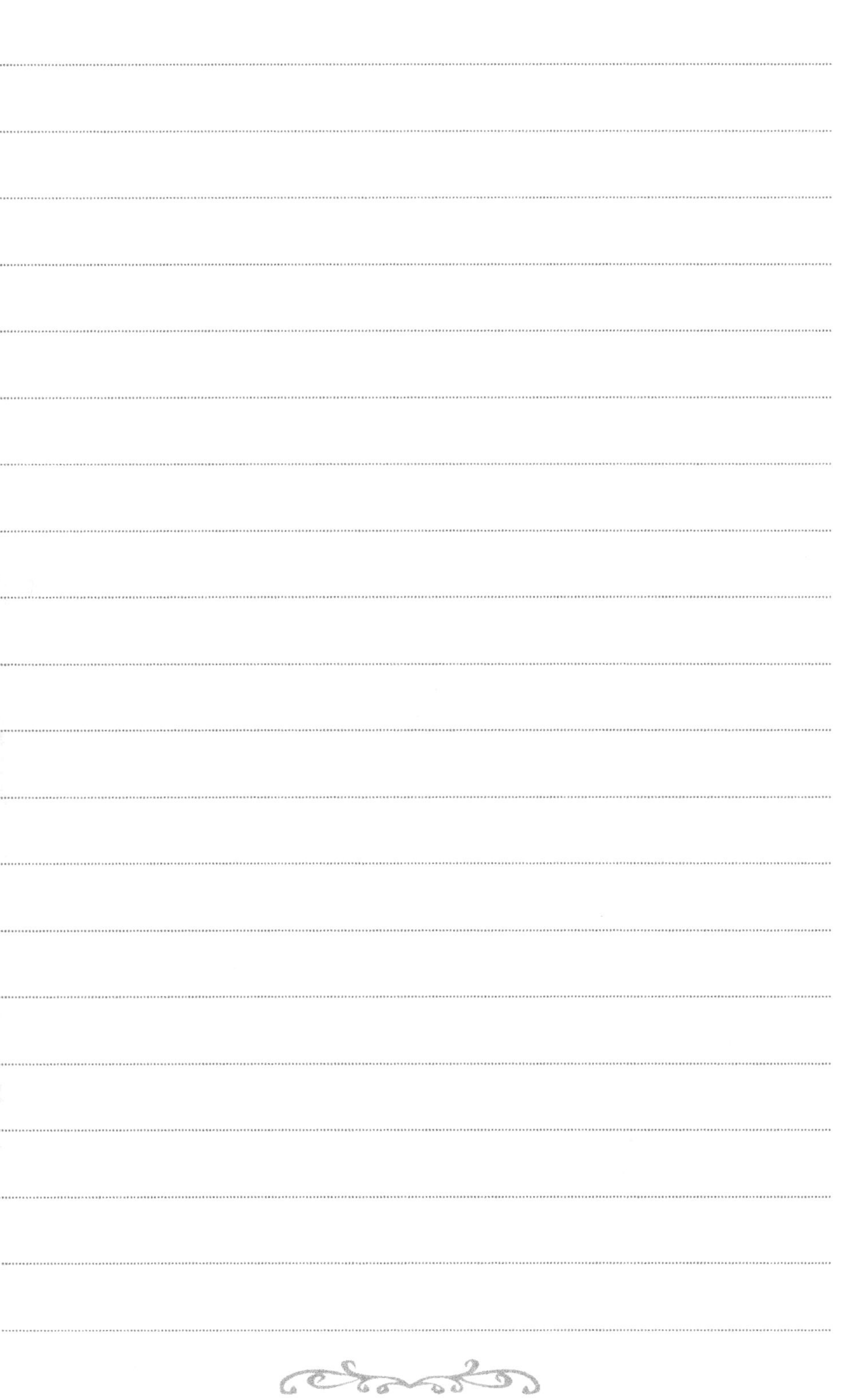

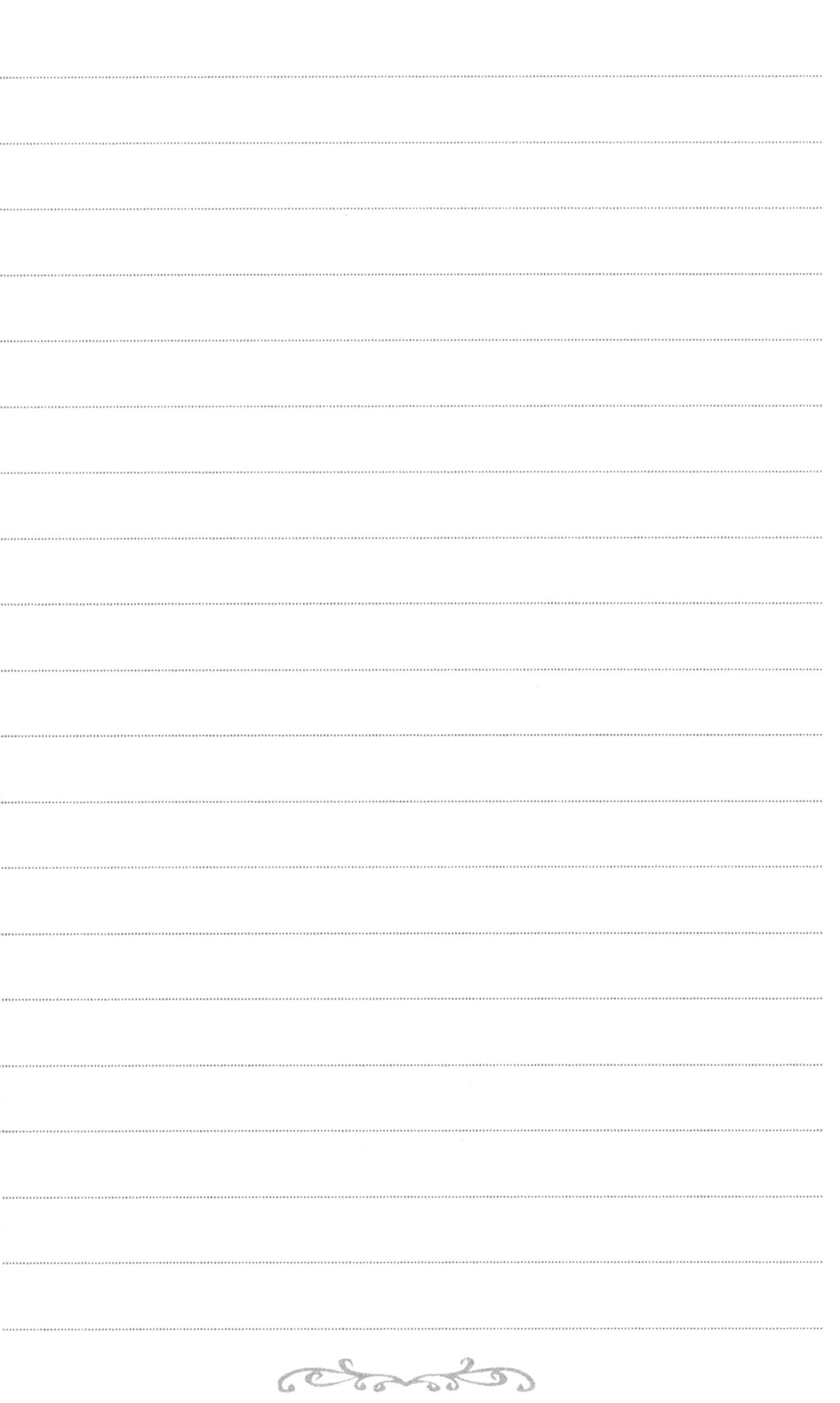

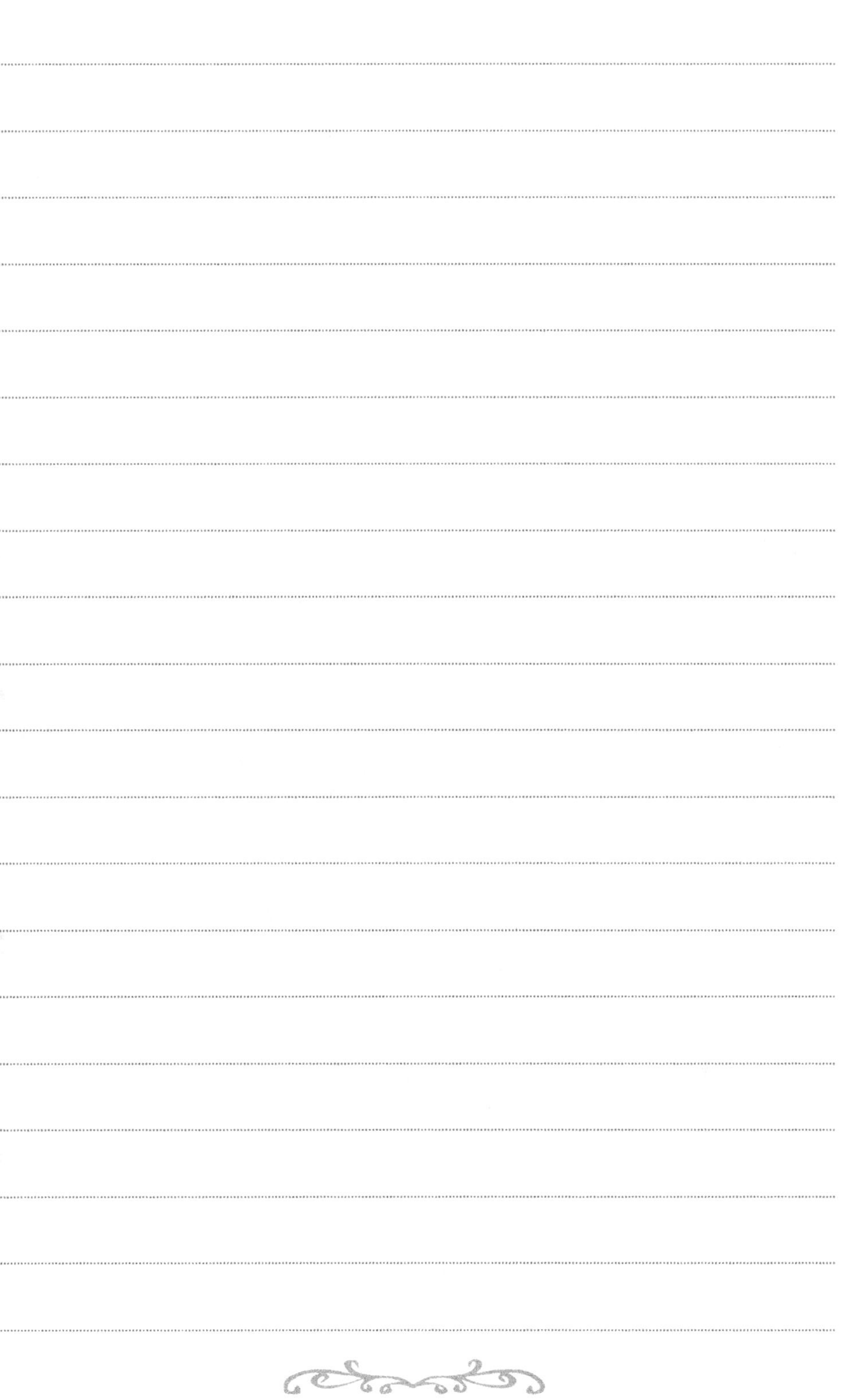

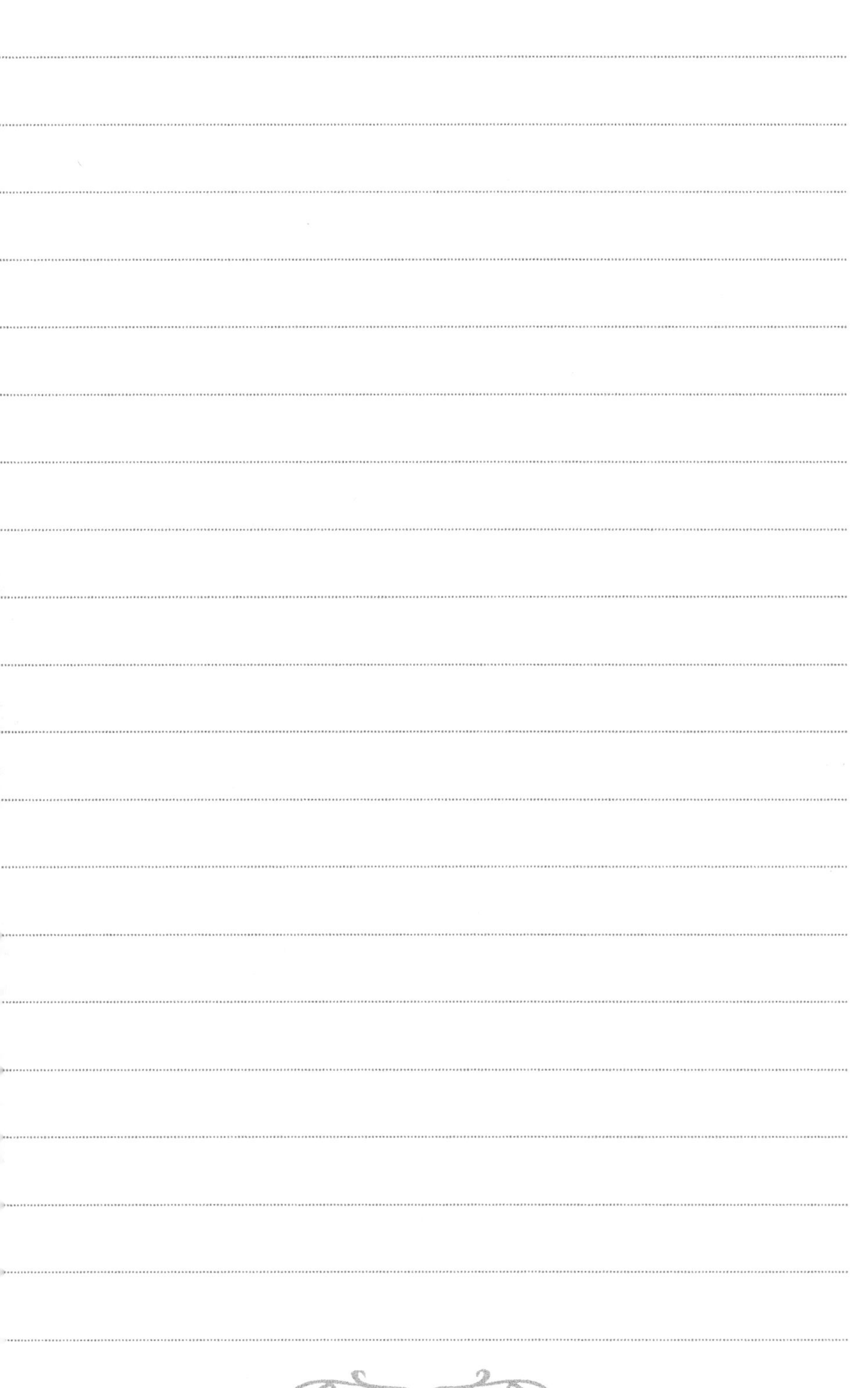

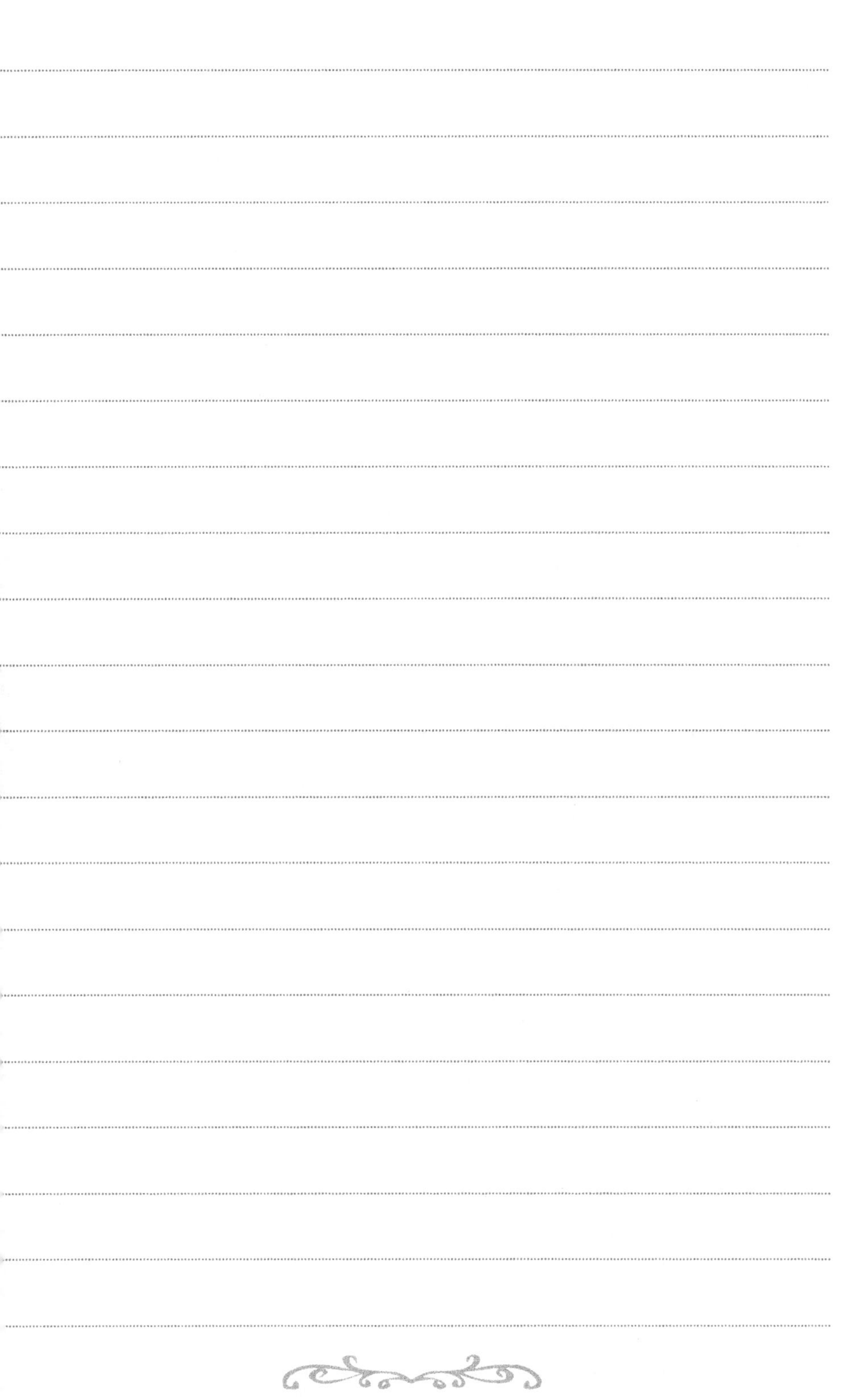

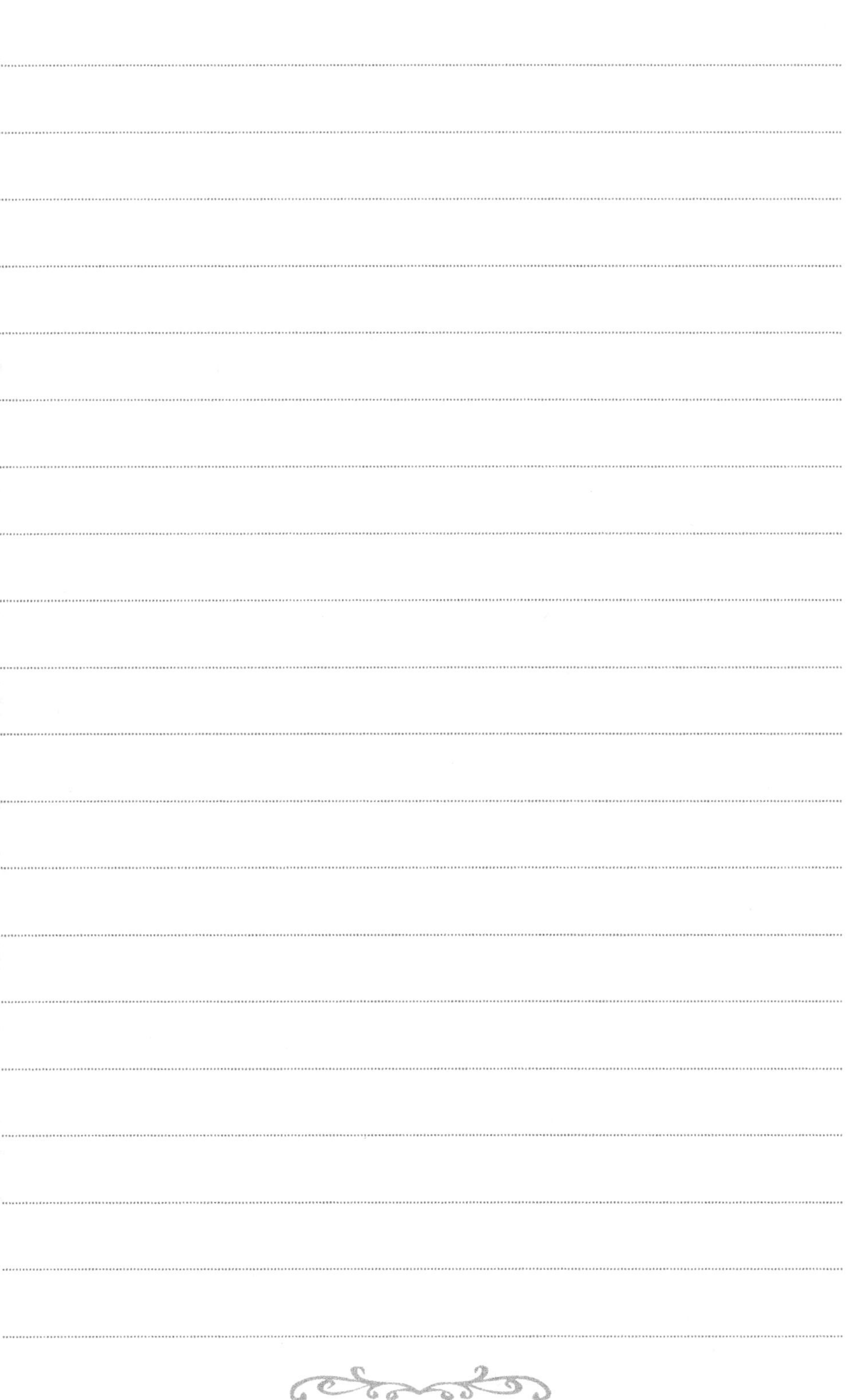

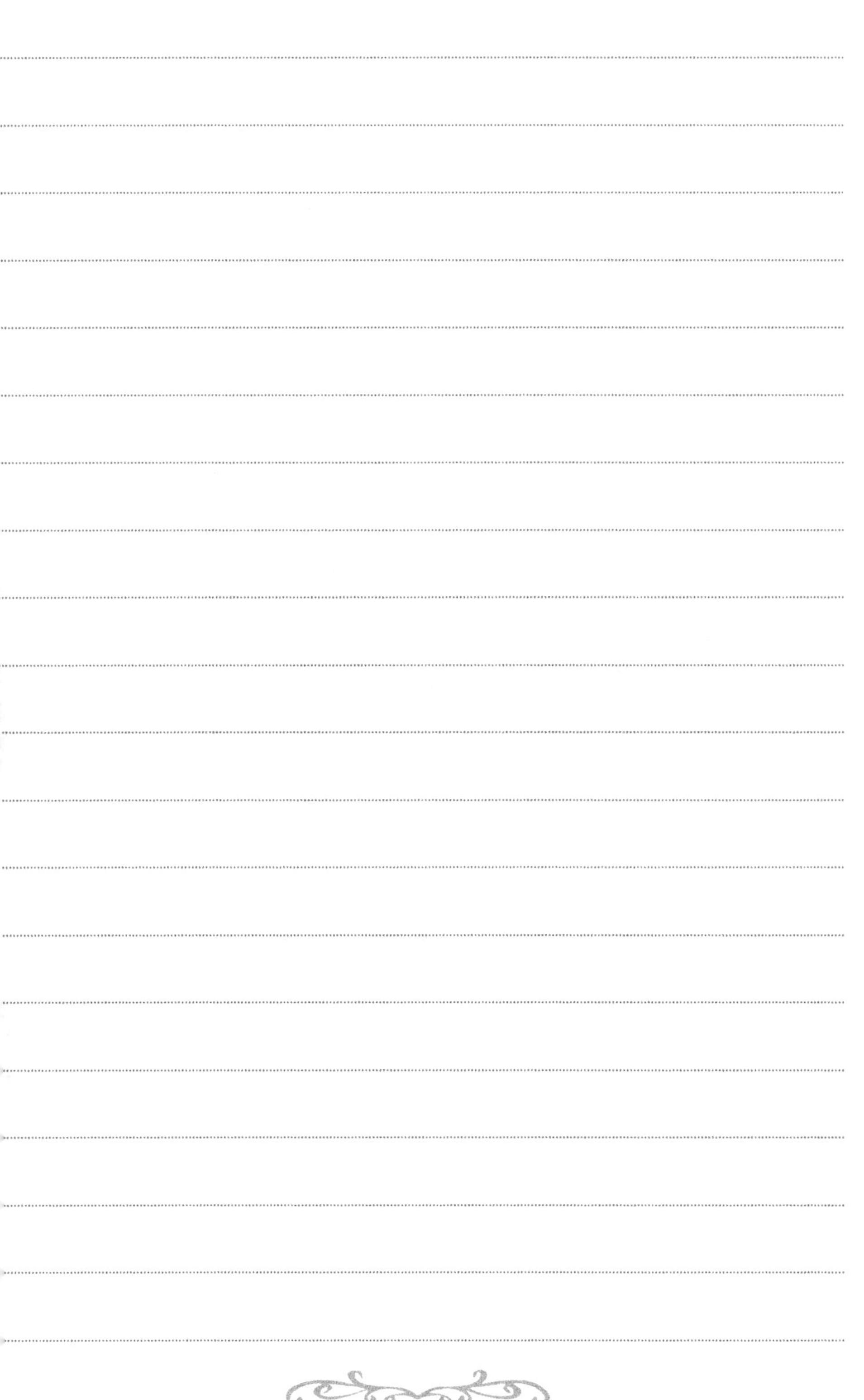

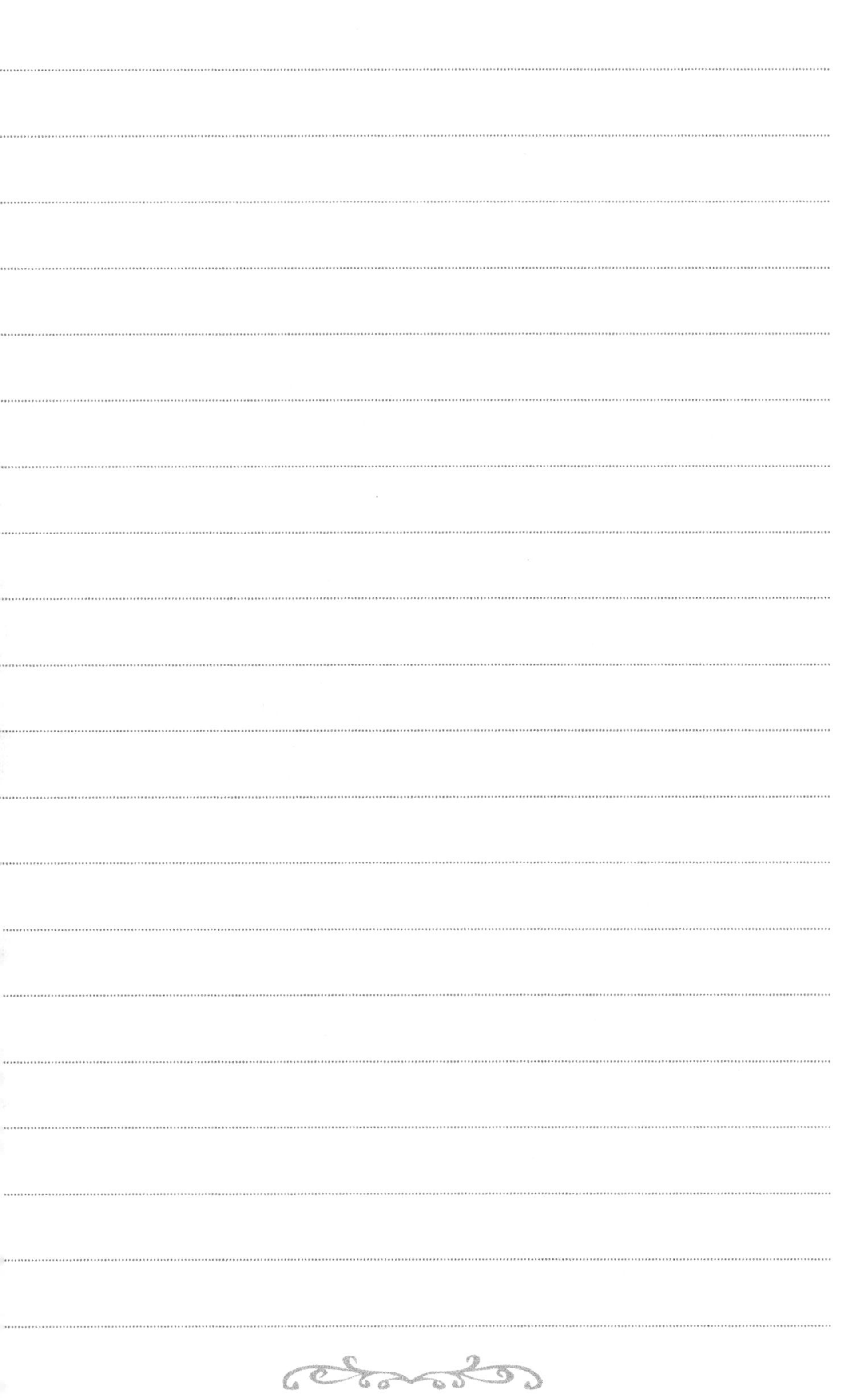

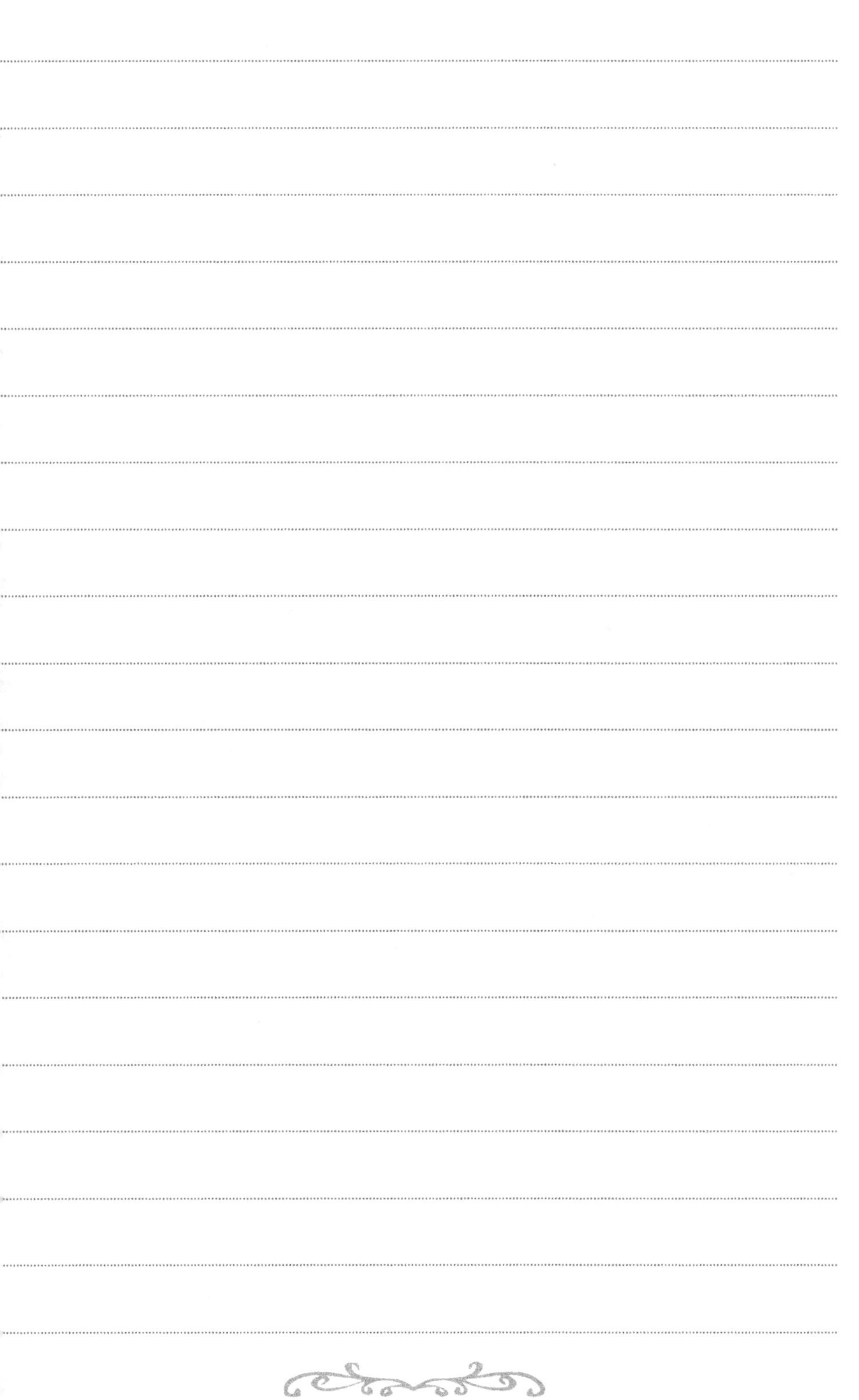

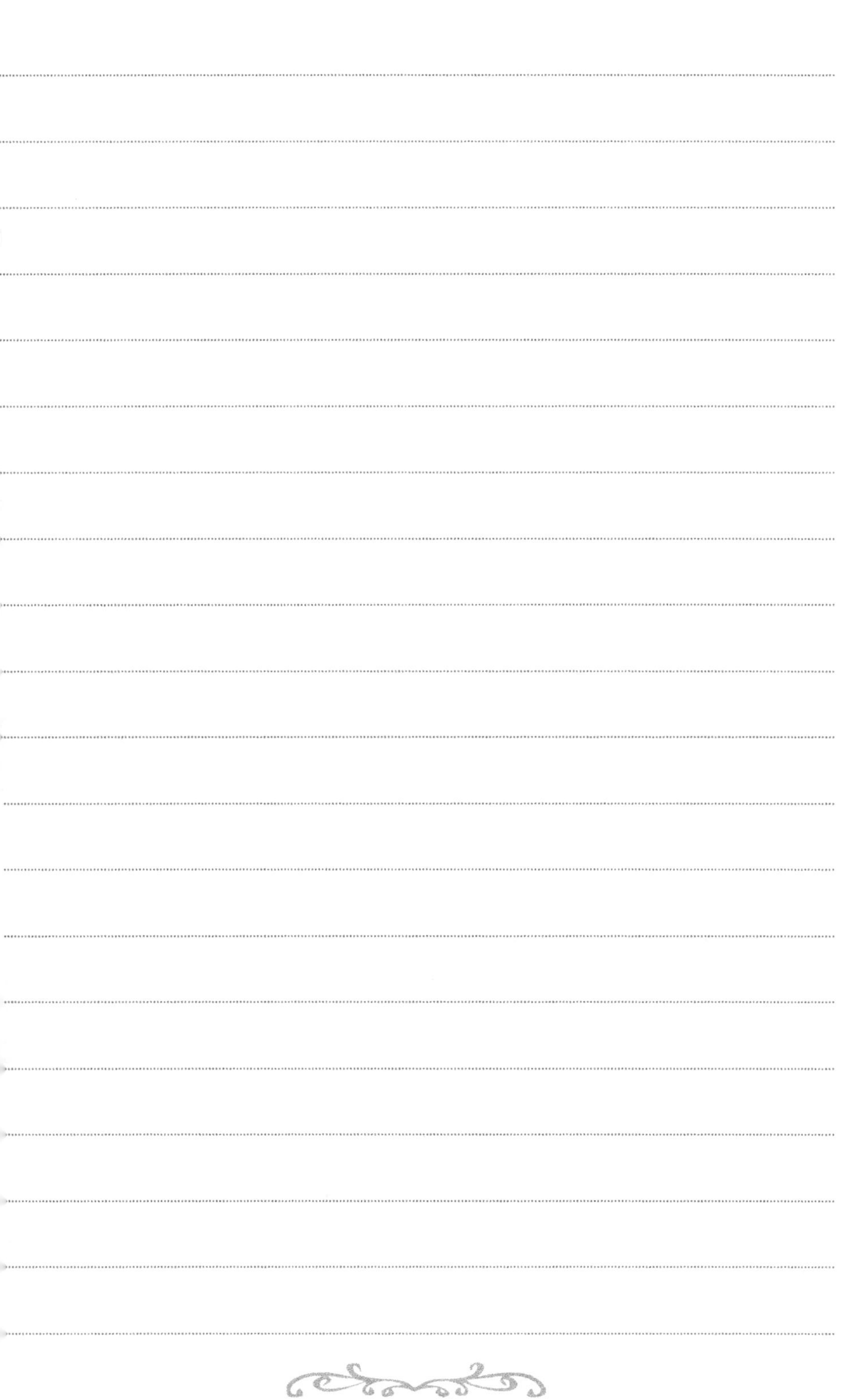

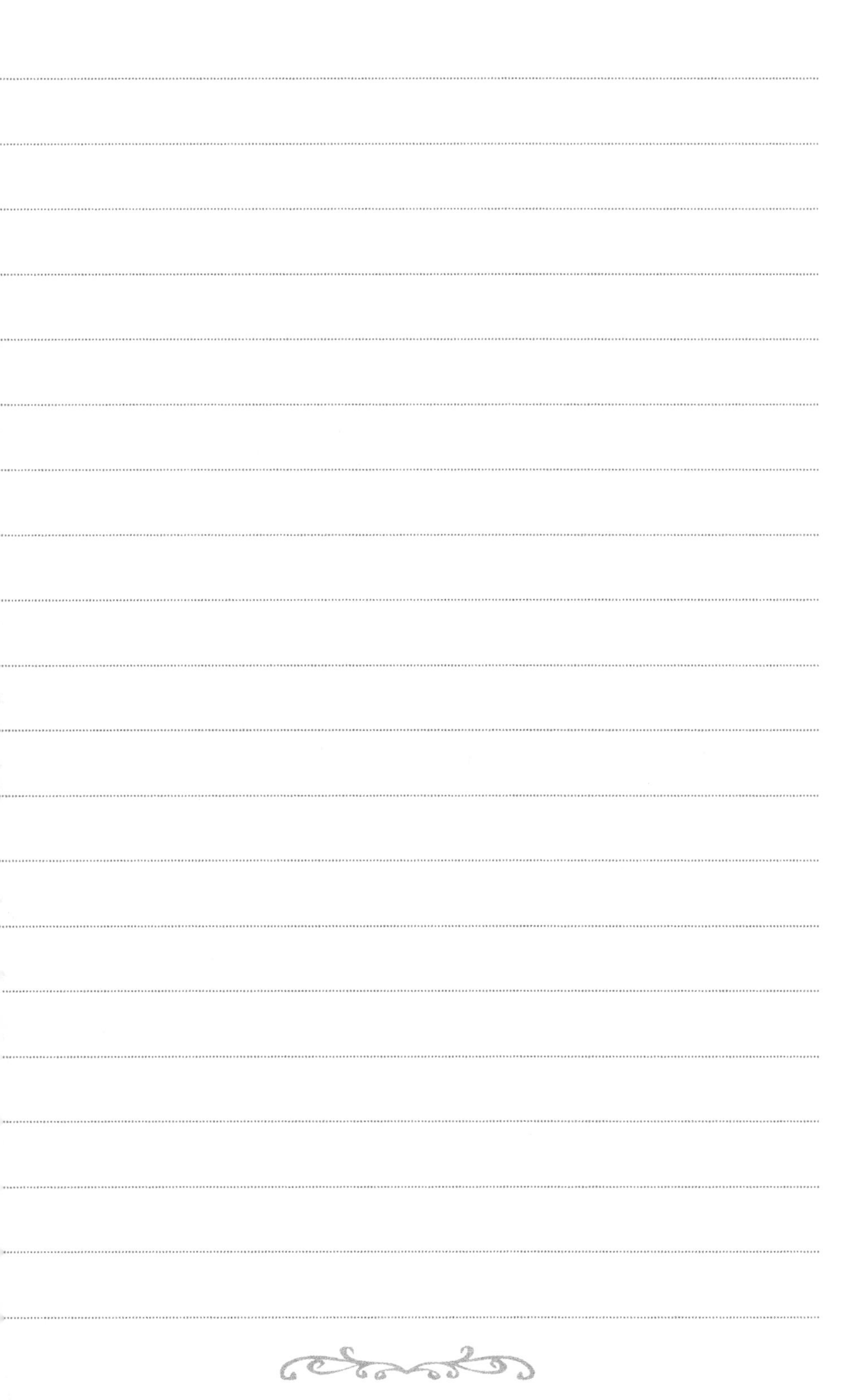

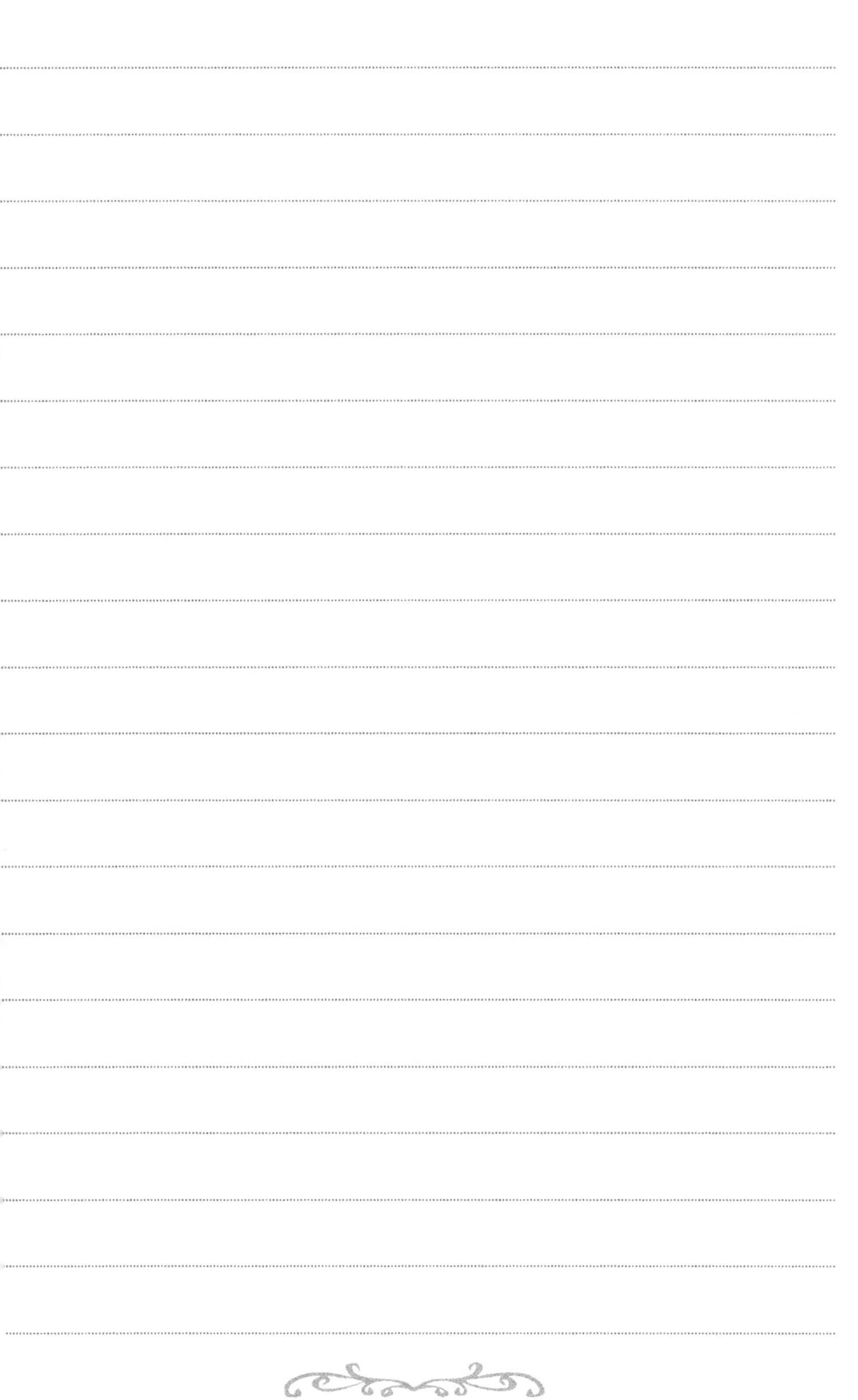

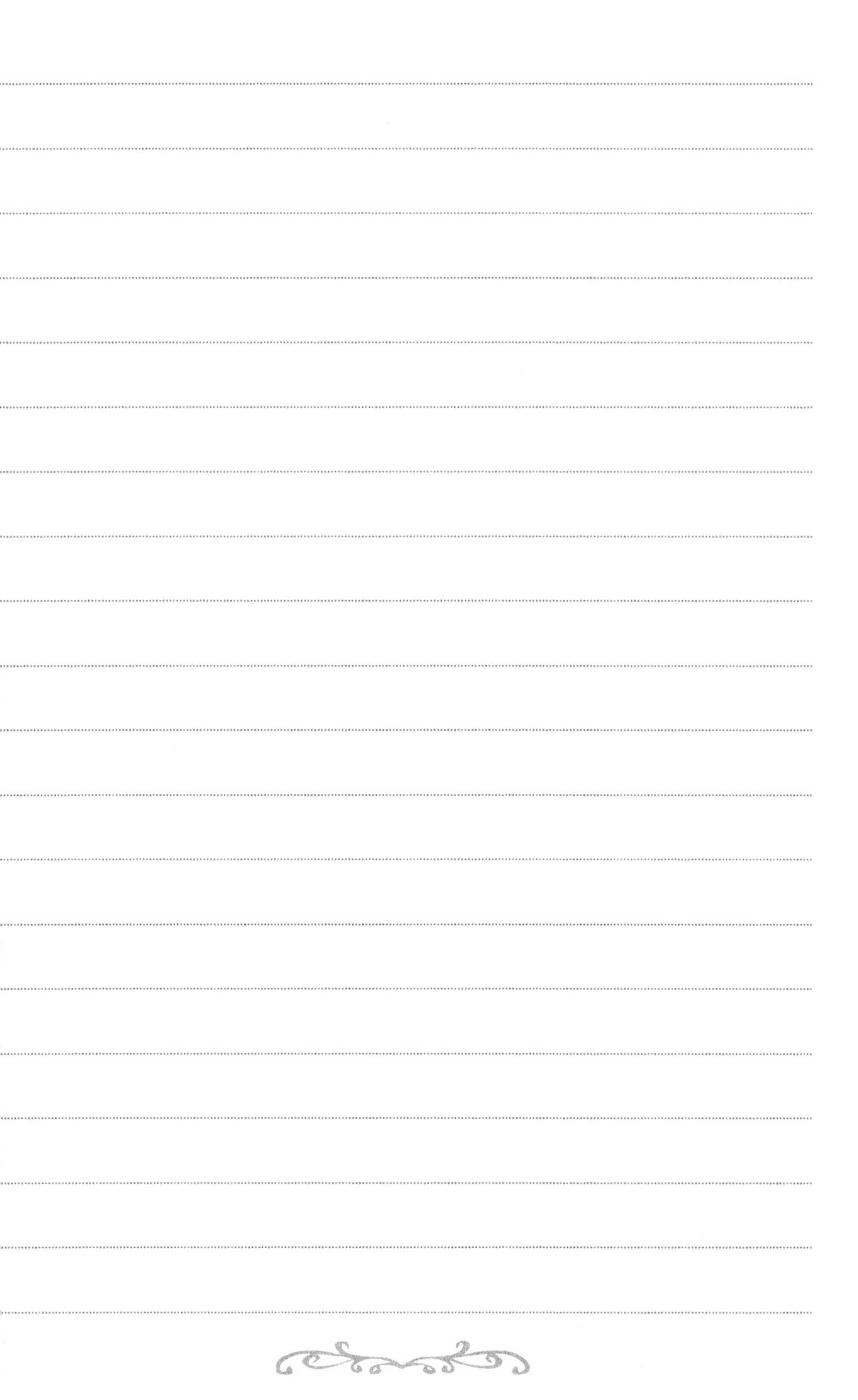

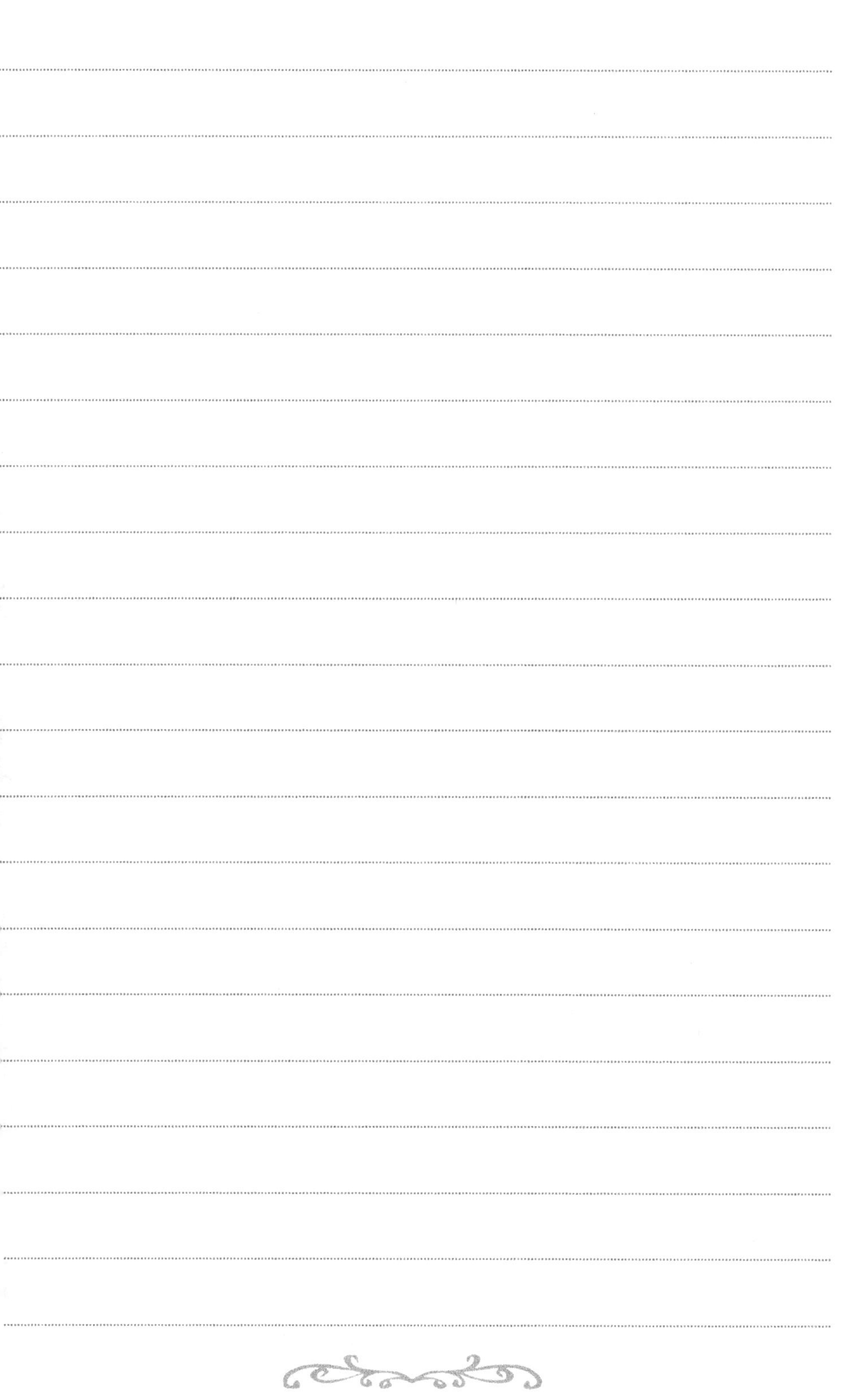

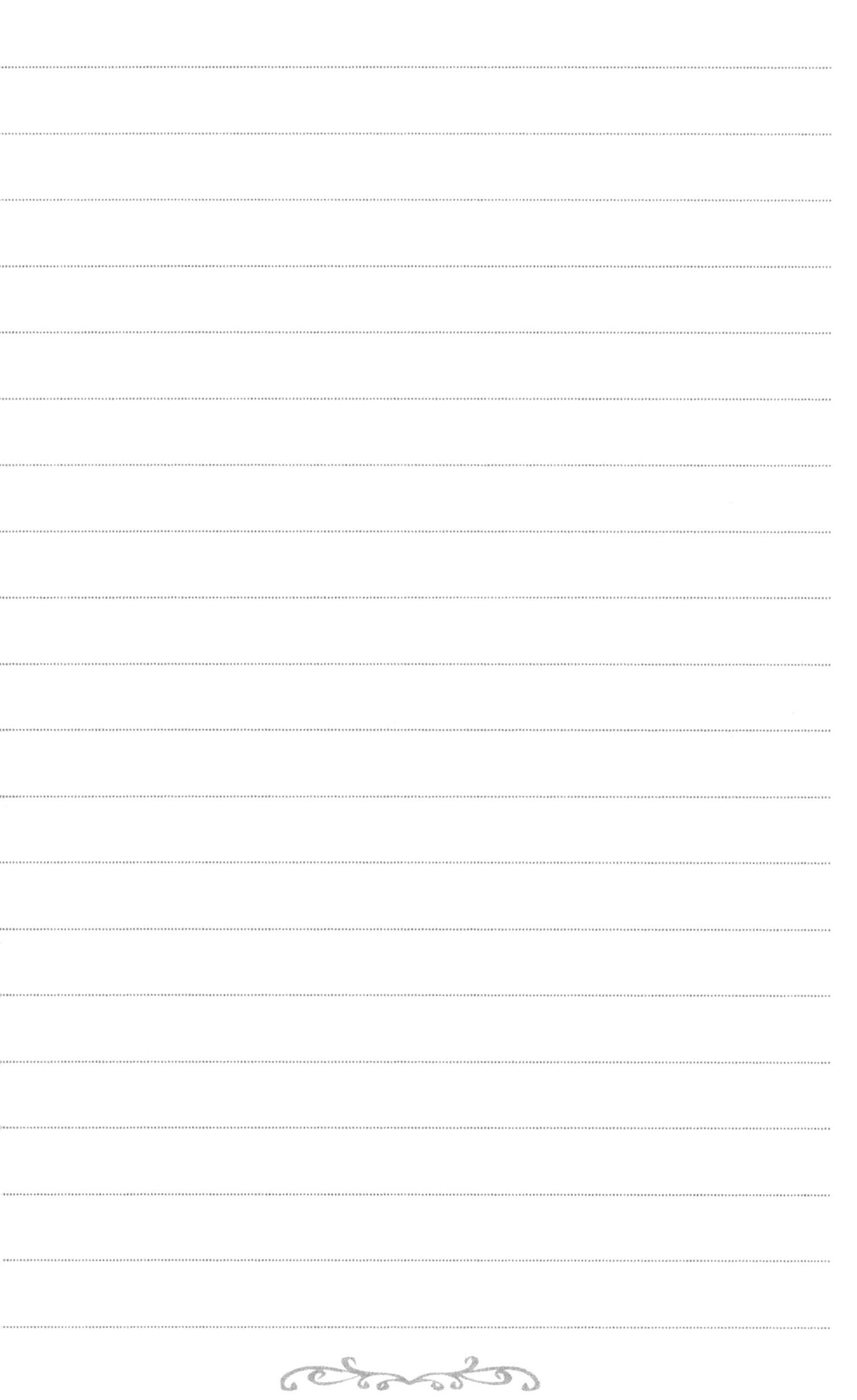

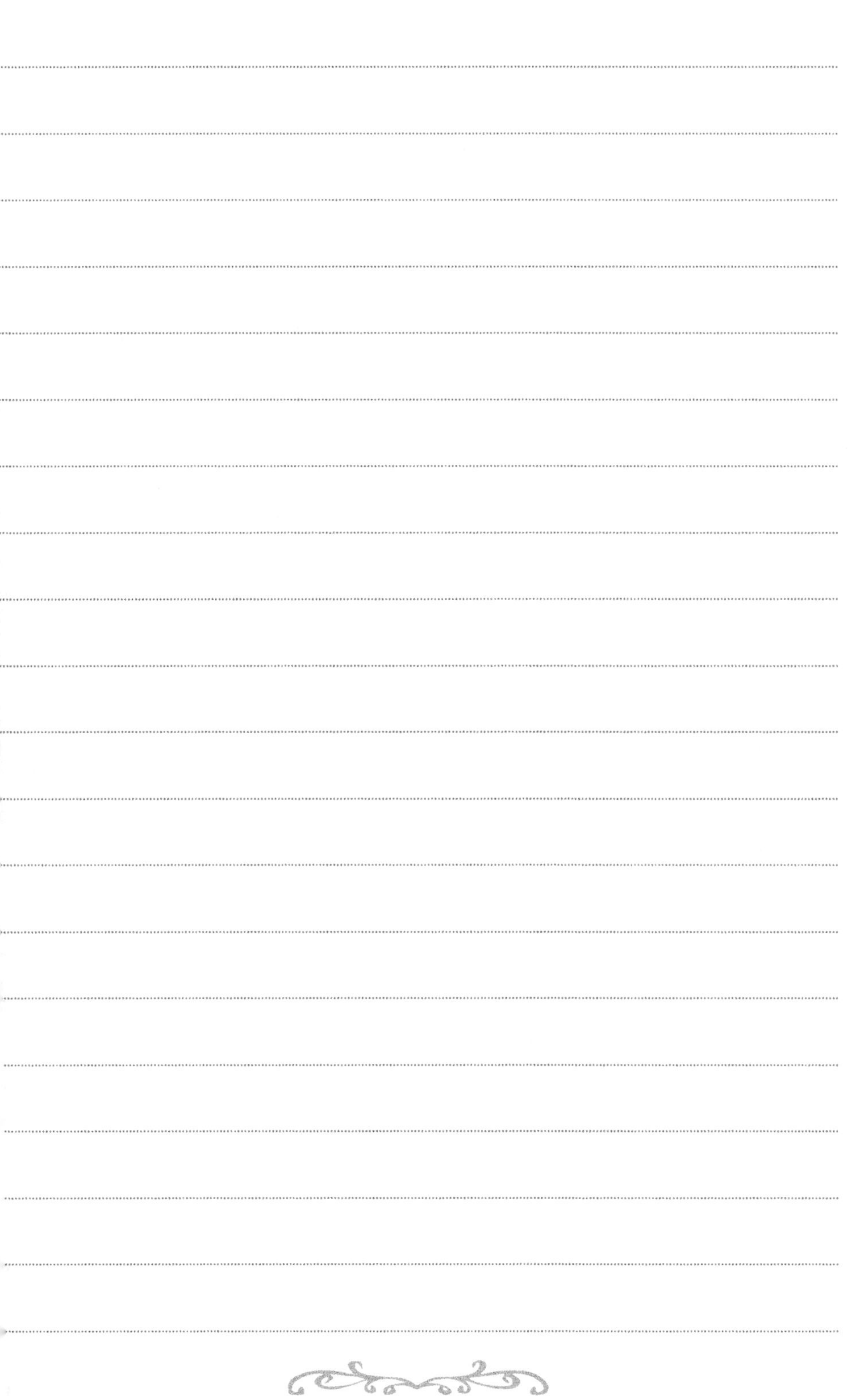

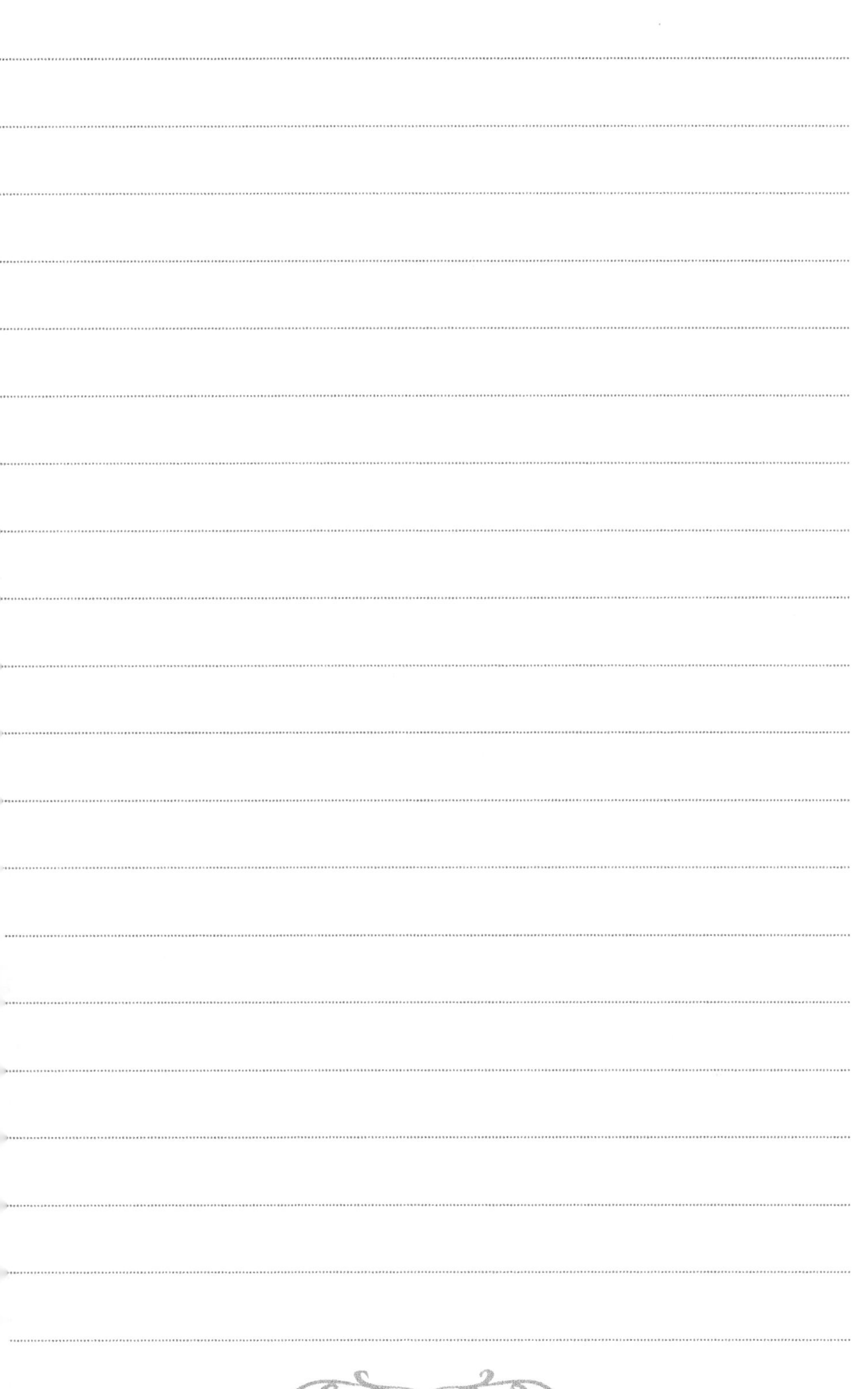

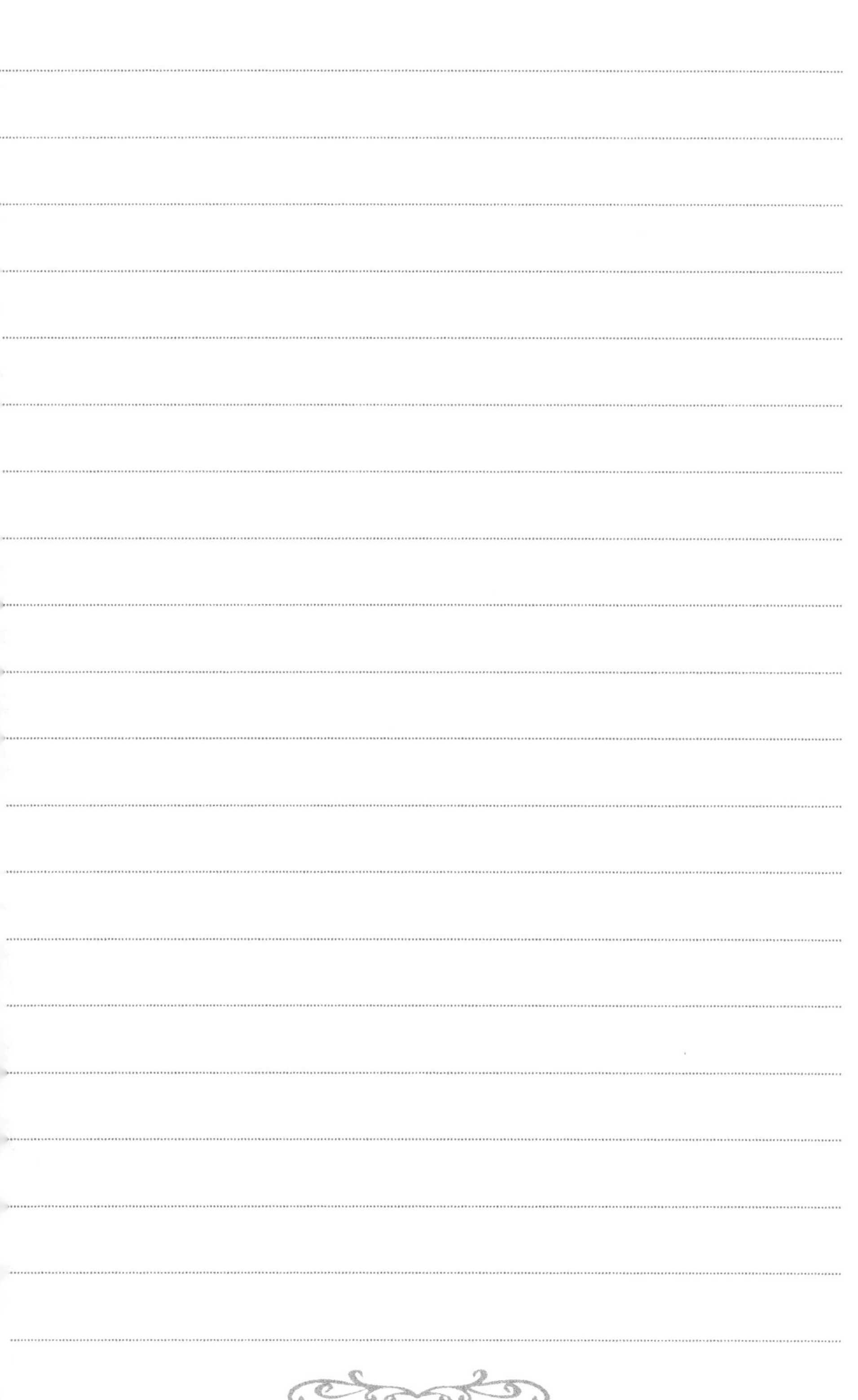

9 798330 232376